Sitting Bull

EAGLES CANNOT BE CROWS

Jody Jensen Shaffer, M.A.

Consultants

Vanessa Ann Gunther, Ph.D.
Department of History
Chapman University

Nicholas Baker, Ed.D.
Supervisor of Curriculum and Instruction
Colonial School District, DE

Katie Blomquist, Ed.S.
Fairfax County Public Schools

Publishing Credits

Rachelle Cracchiolo, M.S.Ed., *Publisher*
Conni Medina, M.A.Ed., *Managing Editor*
Emily R. Smith, M.A.Ed., *Series Developer*
Diana Kenney, M.A.Ed., NBCT, *Content Director*
Courtney Patterson, *Senior Graphic Designer*
Lynette Ordoñez, *Editor*

Image Credits: Cover and p. 1 Hulton Archive/Getty Images; cover Niday Picture Library/Alamy Stock Photo; p. 1 Hulton Archive/Getty Images; p. 2 LOC [LC-DIG-ppmsca-39879]; pp. 4-7 Nancy G Western Photography, Nancy Greifenhagen/Alamy Stock Photo; p. 7 (top) Brooklyn Museum of Art Collection/Bridgeman Images; pp. 8-9, 11, 18 North Wind Picture Archives; p. 9 Heritage Image Partnership Ltd/Alamy Stock Photo; p. 10 LOC [LC-USZ62-117640]; p. 12 LOC [LC-DIG-ppmsca-02887]; p. 13 (top) MPI/Getty Images, (bottom) De Agostini Picture Library/Bridgeman Images; pp. 14, 16, 17, 25 Granger, NYC; p. 15 (top) NARA [299803], (bottom) Walters Art Museum/Wikimedia Commons; p. 18 Kean Collection/Getty Images; p. 19 LOC [LC-DIG-cwpbh-03122]; pp. 20-21 De Agostini Picture Library/Bridgeman Images; p. 21 Chicago History Museum, USA/Bridgeman Images; p. 22 (left) LOC [LC-USZ62-122853], (right) Transcendental Graphics/Getty Images; p. 23 De Agostini Picture Library/Bridgeman Images; p. 24 Bettmann/Getty Images; p. 25 Classic Image/Alamy Stock Photo; pp. 26, 27 (top) Look and Learn/Bridgeman Images; p. 28 (bottom) LOC [LC-DIG-ds-07833]; p. 28 Jozef Klopacka/Alamy Stock Photo; p. 29 (top) The Stapleton Collection/Bridgeman Images, (bottom) Sioux/Detroit Institute of Arts, USA/Bridgeman Images; p. 31 LOC [LC-USZ62-117640]; p. 32 LOC [LC-DIG-ppmsca-39879]; all other images from iStock and/or Shutterstock.

Library of Congress Cataloging-in-Publication Data

Names: Shaffer, Jody Jensen, author.
Title: Sitting Bull : eagles cannot be crows / Jody Jensen Shaffer, M.A.
Description: Huntington Beach, CA : Teacher Created Materials, 2017. | Includes index.
Identifiers: LCCN 2016034145 (print) | LCCN 2016035088 (ebook) | ISBN
  9781493838004 (pbk.) | ISBN 9781480757653 (eBook)
Subjects: LCSH: Sitting Bull, 1831-1890--Juvenile literature. | Dakota
  Indians--Biography--Juvenile literature. | Hunkpapa
  Indians--Biography--Juvenile literature. | Dakota
  Indians--History--Juvenile literature.
Classification: LCC E99.D1 S43 2017 (print) | LCC E99.D1 (ebook) | DDC
  978.004/975243--dc23
LC record available at https://lccn.loc.gov/2016034145

Teacher Created Materials

5301 Oceanus Drive
Huntington Beach, CA 92649-1030
http://www.tcmpub.com

ISBN 978-1-4938-3800-4

Table of Contents

Character Counts

It was a contest all the young boys of the **tribe** wanted to win. Whoever shot the prettiest bird would get a prize. The prize was a bow and a set of arrows made by the arrow maker. Jumping Badger and his friends saw two boys firing at a bird in a tree. One boy's arrow missed the bird and got stuck in a tree limb. It was the boy's favorite arrow. He promised to reward anyone who got it back.

Jumping Badger aimed and knocked the arrow to the ground. But in the process, the arrow broke. The owner said Jumping Badger should pay for it. But Jumping Badger's friends said the boy should keep his promise and should reward him. Jumping Badger did not want to fight. He gave the boy his own favorite arrow.

That night, Jumping Badger's friends told the arrow maker how selfless he had been. The arrow maker gave the prize to Jumping Badger for his generosity. Jumping Badger grew up to be Sitting Bull, a man who was a strong leader throughout his life.

Lakota boy with a bow and arrow

WHAT'S IN A NAME?

At birth, Lakota babies are named for an event in their father's life. Later, they earn an adult name from a deed of their own.

Growing and Learning

Jumping Badger was born around 1831. His exact birthdate is unknown. His family lived on the **Great Plains** in what is now South Dakota. They were members of the Hunkpapa tribe of the Lakota peoples. His mother was Her-Holy-Door, and his father was Sitting Bull. Sitting Bull was one of several **chiefs**. Jumping Badger's family owned many horses, which made them rich by Lakota standards.

Jumping Badger was a thoughtful boy. His careful actions earned him the nickname "Slow." In fact, his friends and family called him Slow for most of his childhood.

Lakota boy with horse

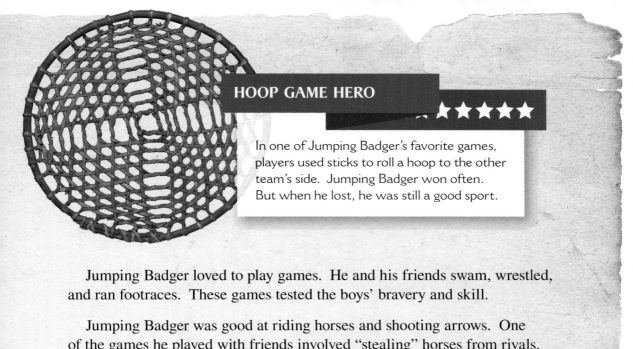

HOOP GAME HERO

★★★★★

In one of Jumping Badger's favorite games, players used sticks to roll a hoop to the other team's side. Jumping Badger won often. But when he lost, he was still a good sport.

Jumping Badger loved to play games. He and his friends swam, wrestled, and ran footraces. These games tested the boys' bravery and skill.

Jumping Badger was good at riding horses and shooting arrows. One of the games he played with friends involved "stealing" horses from rivals. This game was good practice for real life. Enemy tribes often stole each other's horses.

Horses were an important part of Lakota life. The people hunted buffalo on horseback. Buffalo gave the Lakota most of what they needed to live. They used every part of the buffalo for food, clothing, shelter, and tools.

Jumping Badger became a skilled rider and hunter. He killed his first buffalo at age 10. He often gave the buffalo he hunted to families that did not have horses. These generous gifts earned his tribe's respect.

American Indians hunt buffalo

When Jumping Badger was 14, he joined a hunting party in a raid on a Crow tribe. He rode into the group of Crow **warriors** and knocked a man off his horse with a stick. This was called counting coup (COO). It was far more dangerous than shooting an arrow from far away.

Jumping Badger's father was proud of his son's bravery. That night, he held a feast. He painted his son black and gave him a white eagle feather to wear in his hair. He presented a shield that had been made for the young warrior. Finally, he gave Jumping Badger his own name—Sitting Bull.

coup stick

FOUR VIRTUES

The Lakota are taught to embody the four **virtues**: bravery, **fortitude**, generosity, and wisdom. Jumping Badger proved to his tribe that he was brave when he counted first coup.

wisdom

bravery

fortitude

generosity

Natural Leader

As a young man, Sitting Bull was a model of Lakota virtues. He was brave, tough, generous, and wise. On the hunt, he would race up to a buffalo herd and kill several animals before the other hunters caught up. In battle, he was equally bold. Enemies feared the name Sitting Bull. His fellow warriors used this to their advantage. Riding into battle, they would shout, "Sitting Bull, I am he!"

As a young man, Sitting Bull was made a member of the Strong Heart Warrior Society. This was a special group of the bravest warriors. Soon, Sitting Bull became the group's leader.

But Sitting Bull was not just a brave warrior. He was also a spiritual leader. He took part in his first Sun Dance when he was 25. For this important ritual, Sitting Bull pierced his skin with wood pieces tied to ropes. The ropes were fixed to a pole. Sitting Bull danced around the pole for hours in the hot sun. Surviving this painful ritual earned him the title Wichasha Wakan, or holy man.

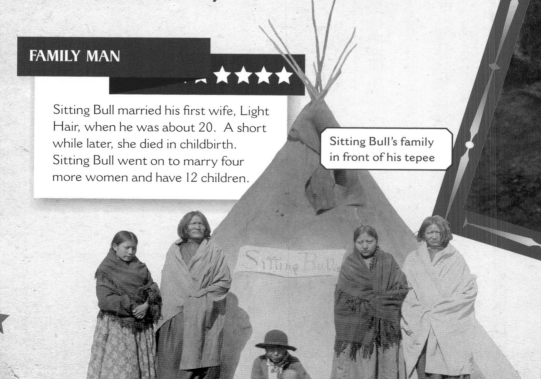

FAMILY MAN

Sitting Bull married his first wife, Light Hair, when he was about 20. A short while later, she died in childbirth. Sitting Bull went on to marry four more women and have 12 children.

Sitting Bull's family in front of his tepee

Sun Dance ritual

Sitting Bull earned the respect of his people. They trusted his leadership in a world that was changing quickly. In the mid-1800s, cities in the East were getting crowded. Land was pricey, and good jobs were hard to find. Many people looked to the West. They saw land that was cheap and often free. They saw room for farms and ranches. They did not consider the rights of the American Indians who already lived there.

Many Americans also believed in **Manifest Destiny**. They said the United States was meant to stretch from ocean to ocean. They saw it as their duty to start schools, build churches, and spread the American way of life.

Sitting Bull and his people had met many white traders. But suddenly, white **settlers** were taking over the land. Many tribes fought back. The U.S. Army sent soldiers to protect the settlers.

In 1862, gold was found in the nearby Rocky Mountains. Miners flooded the region. A few years later, the **Civil War** ended. Many former soldiers headed west. More settlers meant more bloody battles.

Americans travel west in search of new opportunities.

This 1864 poster encourages Americans to fight American Indians.

U.S. troops attack the Cheyenne during the Sand Creek Massacre.

ATTENTION!
INDIAN
FIGHTERS

Having been authorized by the Governor to raise a Company of 100 day
U. S. VOL CAVALRY!

For immediate service against hostile Indians. I call upon all who wish to engage in such service to call at my office and enroll their names immediately.

Pay and Rations the same as other U. S. Volunteer Cavalry.

Parties furnishing their own horses will receive 40c per day, and rations for the same, while in the service.

The Company will also be entitled to all horses and other plunder taken from the Indians.

Office first door East of Recorder's Office.

Central City, Aug. 13, '64.

SAND CREEK MASSACRE

★★★★★★★★

In 1864, U.S. troops attacked a Cheyenne village. The attack became known as the Sand Creek Massacre. A few months later, Sitting Bull agreed to join other Plains Indians to seek revenge. But their weapons were no match for the army's.

In 1868, the U.S. government asked the Lakota and Dakota tribes to sign a **treaty**, or agreement. The Second Treaty of Fort Laramie set aside land for the tribes. This land was called the Great Sioux (SOO) **Reservation**. The government said it would keep white settlers off the land. But they wanted the tribes to stay only on the land set aside for them. They promised food, clothing, and blankets to tribes who signed the treaty.

Lakota and Dakota tribes moved often to follow buffalo herds. Living in a confined area would change their way of life. But that was the government's plan. Many white people saw American Indians as **savages**. They wanted the tribes to be more like them—to settle in one place, speak English, and go to church.

A small number of tribes signed the treaty. These tribes already lived on the land and would not have to move. But Sitting Bull and most other leaders rejected the treaty. Sitting Bull gained the respect of many tribes.

Around this time, Sitting Bull's uncle led a movement to encourage all the Lakota bands to follow Sitting Bull. The Lakota bands had never been united like that before. More people came to seek Sitting Bull's guidance.

signers of the Second Treaty of Fort Laramie

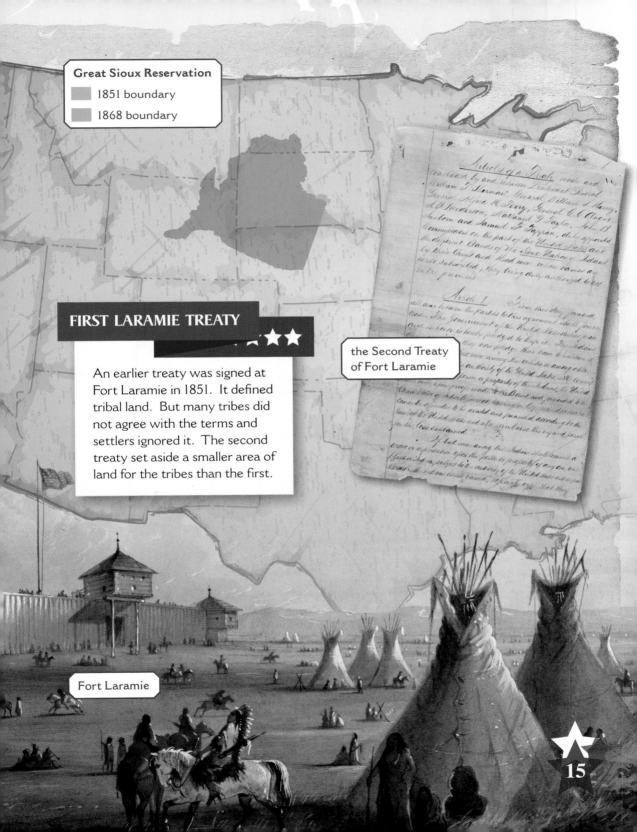

Great Sioux Reservation

■ 1851 boundary
■ 1868 boundary

FIRST LARAMIE TREATY

★ ★

the Second Treaty of Fort Laramie

An earlier treaty was signed at Fort Laramie in 1851. It defined tribal land. But many tribes did not agree with the terms and settlers ignored it. The second treaty set aside a smaller area of land for the tribes than the first.

Fort Laramie

A crew builds a railroad in the Dakota Territory in 1879.

Broken Promises

The treaty promised to keep white settlers off the reservation. But within a few years, railroad workers came to the reservation. They planned to build tracks along the Yellowstone River. The treaty allowed a railroad to be built. But the language of the treaty was confusing. So tribes were upset when construction began.

The railroad workers were guarded by U.S. soldiers. In 1872, fighting broke out between the soldiers and the tribes. During one battle, Sitting Bull and four other men walked onto the battlefield. Bullets whizzed past as they sat in a circle. Sitting Bull's nephew, White Bull, called this "the bravest deed possible."

During the next two years, Sitting Bull's people and U.S. troops clashed several times over the railroad. The tribes used traditional tactics, such as raids on enemy camps. They fought with bows and arrows and guns. The tribes' efforts slowed work on the railroad, but the people could not beat U.S. troops.

Stories about Sitting Bull's brave acts made him a legend among U.S. troops. No longer did they try to get him to sign a treaty.

American Indians capture and raid an American train.

White settlers kill buffalo.

After the Black Hills expedition, thousands of miners claimed land that belonged to the Lakota.

gold nuggets

In 1874, the government broke the treaty. It had long been rumored that there was gold in the Black Hills. The government tried to buy the land, but the tribes refused to sell. The Black Hills are sacred to the Lakota. The mountains are rich in tradition and resources. Sitting Bull said the tribe must never give them up.

So, Lieutenant Colonel (loo-TEN-ehnt KUHR-nuhl) George Armstrong Custer and his troops came to the reservation to see if the rumors were true. Several newspaper reporters came along to spread the word if gold was found.

Custer's men did find gold in the Black Hills. Soon, the region was flooded with **prospectors**. The government decided that the tribes must give up the Black Hills. President Ulysses S. Grant wrote a new treaty. He offered to pay for the land. But the tribes were not interested in money.

As the number of white settlers grew, the buffalo began to disappear. Settlers killed more buffalo than they needed for food. They killed for sport and to force tribes to move. Soon, tribes began to starve. For many people, reservation life now meant survival. But Sitting Bull and his followers refused to surrender.

EXPERIENCED SOLDIER

★★★★★★

George Armstrong Custer was a teacher before he went to West Point military academy. During the Civil War, Custer was a soldier in the Union army. He rose through the ranks to become a lieutenant colonel.

Battles of the Rosebud and the Little Bighorn

Military leaders and American Indian officials met with President Grant in November of 1875. The leaders agreed that the remaining "hunting bands" must be stopped. They set a deadline. By January 31, 1876, these bands had to leave the Black Hills. If they stayed, the U.S. Army would wage war on them.

The deadline passed, and still Sitting Bull, Crazy Horse, and their people did not leave. In mid-March, troops rode into a village of sleeping Lakota families. The soldiers began shooting and burning tepees. The war had begun.

Battle of the Rosebud

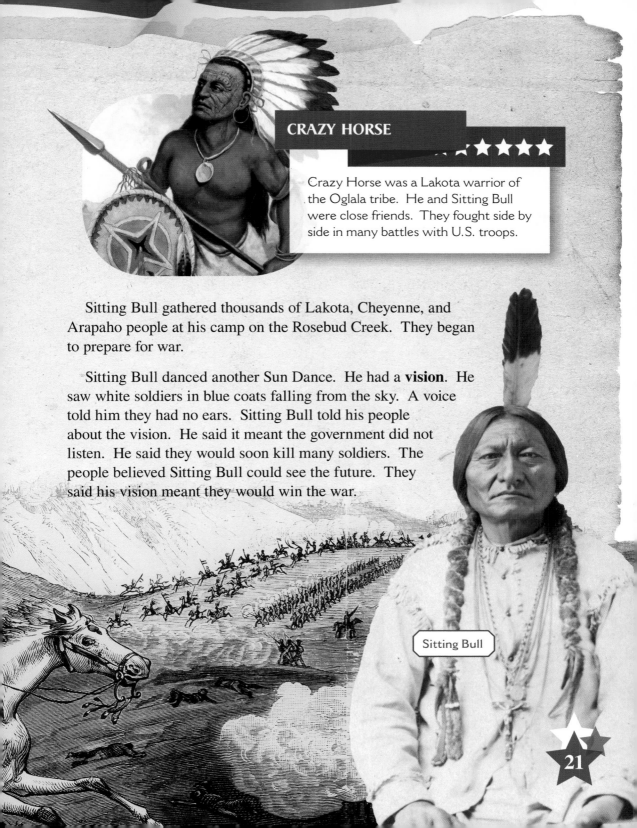

CRAZY HORSE

★★★★

Crazy Horse was a Lakota warrior of the Oglala tribe. He and Sitting Bull were close friends. They fought side by side in many battles with U.S. troops.

Sitting Bull gathered thousands of Lakota, Cheyenne, and Arapaho people at his camp on the Rosebud Creek. They began to prepare for war.

Sitting Bull danced another Sun Dance. He had a **vision**. He saw white soldiers in blue coats falling from the sky. A voice told him they had no ears. Sitting Bull told his people about the vision. He said it meant the government did not listen. He said they would soon kill many soldiers. The people believed Sitting Bull could see the future. They said his vision meant they would win the war.

Sitting Bull

A few days after Sitting Bull's vision, a group of hunters went in search of buffalo. They saw U.S. troops near the camp. Crazy Horse acted quickly. He and his warriors attacked the soldiers. The warriors rode between the soldiers. They leaned over the sides of their horses so they could not be shot. This surprised the soldiers, so they retreated. Crazy Horse thought Sitting Bull's vision had come true. But Sitting Bull said this was not the battle he had seen.

The tribes moved to the valley of the Little Bighorn River. They were joined by more people, some of whom had left the reservation to follow Sitting Bull. Nearly 1,800 American Indians gathered to prepare for battle.

On June 25, 1876, the U.S. Seventh **Cavalry** attacked the camp. Lieutenant Colonel Custer led the charge of more than 200 men. The warriors jumped onto their horses and fought fiercely. They drove the soldiers to a ridge and surrounded them. They killed Custer and all his men. This battle is remembered as Custer's Last Stand.

One Bull

White Bull

TAKING A STEP BACK

Sitting Bull didn't lead the charge at the Battle of the Little Bighorn. He was not a young warrior anymore. He sent his nephew, White Bull, and his adopted son, One Bull, to fight instead.

Battle of the Little Bighorn

To Canada and Back

News of the Battle of the Little Bighorn spread quickly. People could not believe Sitting Bull's warriors had defeated the U.S. Army. More soldiers were sent out to capture the hunting bands. The government took over the Black Hills.

Sitting Bull led his people into Canada in 1877. There were plenty of buffalo, and the people were safe from U.S. troops. Thousands more soon joined them.

Canada began to have doubts about the newcomers. The country had local tribes who also needed buffalo. And it did not want to anger its neighbor to the south. Meanwhile, the tribes were also having a hard time. Winters in Canada were hard. Many people got sick. Thousands moved back to the Great Sioux Reservation.

Sitting Bull saw no choice. In 1881, he surrendered to the United States. He and his family were sent to live in a cabin at Standing Rock in South Dakota. Two years later, the government broke the Great Sioux Reservation into six smaller reservations. This allowed the government to take even more land for the white settlers.

Sitting Bull and his people ask the Canadians for help at Fort Walsh in 1877.

This 1877 political cartoon shows American Indian tribes moving to Canada.

Sitting Bull's cabin at Standing Rock

A Sad End

Living on the reservation was hard. The Lakota had given up their way of life. Some people looked to a new ritual for hope. That ritual was the Ghost Dance. It mixed their traditional beliefs with Christian teachings. Believers said that if they did the Ghost Dance, new land would be filled with buffalo, good soil, and family members who had died in previous wars. When white settlers heard about the Ghost Dance, they were afraid. They thought the dance would lead to violence. They demanded that the U.S. government protect them.

Government officials worked with tribal police to stop the Ghost Dance. On December 15, 1890, Lakota police officers went to Sitting Bull's cabin. They were there to arrest him for supporting the Ghost Dances. Sitting Bull had never participated in the Ghost Dance. But as chief, he took the blame for his people's actions. When police led Sitting Bull from his house, a fight broke out. Sitting Bull was shot and killed by a lawman.

Sitting Bull is remembered as a brave warrior, a powerful leader, and a great **statesman**. He embodied Lakota virtues. He defended them as settlers threatened their way of life. His story continues to inspire people today.

FAMOUS WORDS

★★★★

In 1883, Sitting Bull famously said: "If the Great Spirit had desired me to be a white man, he would have made me so in the first place....Each man is good in his sight. It is not necessary for eagles to be crows."

Ghost Dance

CELEBRITY CHIEF

★★★★★★

During his time on the reservation, Sitting Bull gave newspaper interviews and speeches about his life. He even rode his horse in Buffalo Bill's Wild West Show. This outdoor performance showed life in the Wild West, though it was not entirely accurate. It featured sharp shooters, skilled riders, and battle reenactments.

Draw It!

The Lakota did not have a written language. So, Sitting Bull recorded key events in his life through drawings. He used them to remember events long passed.

Choose an event in Sitting Bull's life. It could be from his childhood, a hunt or raid on an enemy tribe, or a battle with American forces. Draw pictures to tell about this event. Include as many details as you can. Then, write a caption explaining the event.

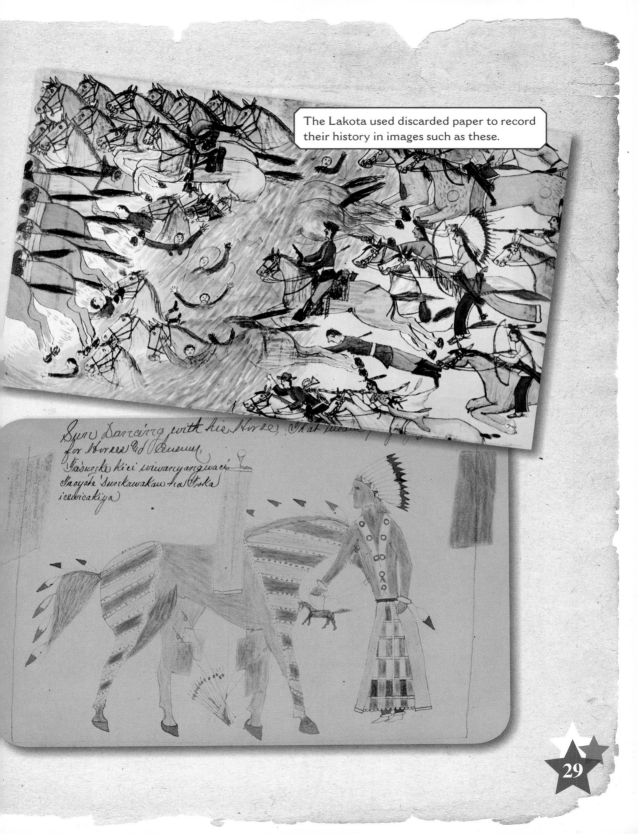

The Lakota used discarded paper to record their history in images such as these.

Glossary

cavalry—an army unit of soldiers that ride horses

chiefs—leaders or rulers of groups of people

Civil War—an American war fought between Northern and Southern states

fortitude—strength and courage that allow a person to face danger or pain

Great Plains—the flat land that lies west of the Mississippi River and east of the Rocky Mountains in the United States and Canada

Manifest Destiny—the idea that the United States had a right to extend its borders to the Pacific Ocean

prospectors—people who search an area for gold, minerals, or oil

reservation—land set aside especially for American Indians to live and work

savages—brutal, rude, and uncivilized people

settlers—people who go to a new place to live

statesman—a respected government leader

treaty—a formal agreement made between two or more countries or groups

tribe—a group of people who have the same language, customs, and beliefs

virtues—good qualities

vision—something that you see or dream, especially as part of a religious or supernatural experience

warriors—people who fight and have courage

Index

Your Turn!

The Life of a Warrior

Sitting Bull was a warrior who fought bravely for his people and his land. He embodied Lakota values and earned the respect of his people. He became a leader in his tribe. Create an illustrated time line of the important events in Sitting Bull's life. Write a caption for each illustration explaining why the event was important. Share your work with your friends and family.